GLENN VAN EKEREN

CELEBRATE

LIVING THE LIFE
YOU'VE IMAGINED

HIGHERLIFE
DEVELOPMENT SERVICES, INC

Celebrate: Living the Life You've Imagined
by Glenn Van Ekeren

Published by HigherLife Publishing and Marketing
400 Fontana Circle Building 1, Suite 105
Oviedo, Florida 32765
(407) 563-4806
www.ahigherlife.com

ISBN 13: 978-1-939183-27-9

Cover Design: Doni Keene

First Edition

14 15 16 17 18 — 9 8 7 6 5 4 3 2 1
Printed in the United States of America

DEDICATION

This book is dedicated to my wife Marty, who lives life to the fullest. It is also dedicated to my children and their spouses for bringing incredible joy into our lives. And finally, to my grandchildren in hopes that they will discover the life God intends for them to live.

TABLE OF CONTENTS

CHAPTER 1

GET IN THE GOOD LIFE NOW

W HAT DAY OF the year did I always wake up early as a kid? Christmas Morning! I loved Christmas morning!

Why?

Dah! Presents.

When I went to bed Christmas Eve, I knew tomorrow was going to be a great day. I believed, without a doubt, my parents had found the perfect present for me and I couldn't wait to unwrap it to see what it was. Positive anticipation prompted me to get out of bed.

How does the Christmas morning experience compare to the way you woke up this morning? What does Christmas morning have to do with living the good life?

What if we viewed each new day as a specially selected gift for us to unwrap and discover? We might be on to something.

Let me draw from the wisdom of a few wise people to provide a glimpse of what might help us experience the Good Life. Mark Twain lamented, "I can teach anybody how to get what they want out of life. The problem is that I can't find anybody who can tell me what they want."

How true, Mr. Twain! It would be a lot easier to achieve what you want out of life if you knew what it was you wanted. If you get up in the morning excited about starting all over again, congratulations! If you're looking to drag your way through another day, my condolences!

The good life is when you wake up in the morning and can't wait to start all over again.

Figure out what you want and you're well on your way to the Good Life.

I thoroughly enjoyed watching Payne Stewart play golf. His flamboyant outfits, highlighted by knickers along with his equally flamboyant personality, complemented by his passion for the game, endeared many fans. Payne definitely stood out from the norm. So did his attitude about life.

Payne once reflected, "I'm going to a special place when I die, but I want to make sure my life is special while I'm here."

I once heard someone describe their life like this, "Each day is just yesterday warmed up!" Same old people. Same old problems. Same old work. All just disguised a little differently than the day before. That is not the kind of 'special' Payne Stewart was referring to.

There is a mental, emotional, physical and spiritual aptitude difference between each day being 'special' and yesterday's leftovers 'reheated'. The best part is...we get to determine what our aptitude will be.

Choose carefully.

Roger Dawson said, "Good things don't happen to you. Bad things don't happen to you. Life is what happens to you. The more you examine the events in your life and categorize them into good things and bad things, the more messed up you're going to become."

Life isn't good! Life isn't bad! Life is life! Stuff happens!

One day, Joe came home from work and his wife greeted him with a passionate hug and warm kiss. "I've got good news and bad news," she said as they ended the embrace.

Joe swallowed hard and suggested she give him the good news first.

> The good life, as I conceive it, is a happy life. I do not mean that if you are good you will be happy; I mean that if you are happy you will be good.
> —BERTRAND RUSSELL

His wife managed a slight smile as she said, "The good news is, the air bag works."

Circumstances do not determine the Good Life or lack of it. Capitalize on the knowledge, insight and wisdom gained from these valuable experiences as a springboard to thinking about how you want things to be.

Ruth Boorstin reminded us, "Our days are identical suitcases – all the same size – but some people pack more into them than others."

Pack your suitcase with good life 'stuff'.

LIVING THE IDEAL

In my early years, happiness was certainly a pursuit. Then, I realized happiness was a fleeting emotion and frankly, I was responsible for my level of happiness. Comfort. That was another priority for a while. Boring! The desire for security slowly evolved into a willingness to explore new ideas, adventures and approaches. You get the idea.

I want to live in a way that counts, that stands for something, that makes some difference. I'll admit I haven't figured it all out, but I know it will require a daily reigniting of commitment and energy to live above the daily grind, the ordinary.

What would your ideal life look like? What does your current life look like? How does it compare to the ideal? What are the gaps? How far apart is the ideal from the real?

Think about this – our life will become exactly what we decide it to be and we will experience what we want most. You might say, "Wait a minute. My life is nothing like I want it to be. In fact, I'm experiencing far from what I want and even farther from the ideal."

I understand. And, I would respond, "If that is true, what action are you taking to close the gap between the real and the ideal? What is your vision for the future?" You show me your vision, and I can predict your future.

Listen (or read) carefully. There are people who are chained to their past and therefore never create a fresh outlook for the future. Other people are so caught up thinking about the future, they fail to take care of the present.

I've learned the past is a marvelous and sometimes painful teacher, the present is filled with opportunity and the future is not something to be feared but enthusiastically pursued.

Without a vision for the future, you will be trapped by the ensnarling enemy called "average" or "good enough".

Without a solid purpose, it is difficult to wrap your arms around a vision that makes sense. When you establish a purpose for your life, it will shape your vision for the future, give you a desire to make significant things happen in your life and instill a desire to change the way things are.

> I cannot believe that the purpose of life is to be 'happy.' I think the purpose of life is to be useful, to be responsible, to be compassionate. It is above all, to matter; to count, to stand for something, to have made some difference that you lived at all.
>
> —LEO CALVIN ROSTEN

The ideal life is a life that revolves around a purpose. God is pleased when you are doing what He designed you to do. Take it from Bertrice Berry who said, "When you walk with purpose, you collide with destiny."

Are you striving to just make it through each day? Are you dreaming about a different kind of life but don't really have any direction? Are you unclear about the difference you can make in other people's lives? Is there a reason for you to get up in the morning beyond the need to make a living?

If you want your life to be something different than it is, then you are going to have to do something different than you've ever done. It has been said that, "Unhappiness is <u>not</u> knowing what we want and killing ourselves to get it."

Listen to Luci Swindoll: "To experience happiness we must train ourselves to live in this moment, to savor it for what it is, not running ahead in anticipation of some future date nor lagging behind in paralysis of the past."

The "good life" is now! This day. This experience. This moment.

CHAPTER 2

FIND YOUR ONE THING

ONE OF THE main reasons why people get stuck and can't go on in life is that they lose vision for what they are to do in the future. We will naturally move forward toward our dreams.

Pulitzer Prize winner, Katherine Anne Porter, said, "I am appalled at the aimlessness of most people's lives. Fifty percent don't pay attention to where they are going; forty percent are undecided and will go in any direction. Only ten percent know what they want, and even all of them don't go toward it."

If you've seen the movie *City Slickers*, you probably recall a memorable scene involving Billy Crystal, who played a city slicker enduring a dude ranch vacation, and Jack Palance, who played a crusty old trail boss.

Here's the scenario. Palance and Crystal are riding slowly across the terrain on horseback, discussing life and love. Crystal is amazed at Palance's apparent ability to enjoy his seemingly questionable, less than exciting life and have his act together while Crystal is struggling to find direction and meaning. Here's their conversation:

Palance: "How old are you? Thirty-eight?"

Crystal:	"Thirty-nine."
Palance:	"Yeah. You all come out here about the same age. Same problems. Spend fifty weeks a year getting knots in your rope -- then you think two weeks up here will untie them for you. None of you get it. [Long pause] Do you know what the secret of life is?"
Crystal:	"No, what?"
Palance:	"It's this." [Holds up his index finger]
Crystal:	"Your finger?"
Palance:	"One thing. Just one thing. You stick to that and everything else don't mean nothing."
Crystal:	"That's great, but what's the one thing?"
Palance:	"That's what you've got to figure out."

The weather-beaten, crusty old cattle driver nailed it. He wasn't verbally elegant, but he was profound and well-seasoned on life's necessities. That one thing is what you've got to figure out.

Don't make this too philosophical. Simply, what is your reason for living? What is your ultimate aim? Why are you here? What is that "one thing" you want to be the driving force for everything you do? If you've never thought about such questions before, you will find the process stimulating and enlightening.

If you have your purpose or your "one thing" in hand, it's the journey that really matters. But, it's the purpose that directs the journey. They're Siamese twins. Purpose and journey.

My simple purpose in life is "to positively impact the lives of people." I shudder to think of the number of times I've fallen short of this lofty ideal. But one thing I know, the more I fulfill that simple purpose, the more I enjoy the journey.

THE FUTURE IS HERE BEFORE YOU KNOW IT

If you are focused on that one thing, your purpose, it's inevitable that your journey will eventually take you to your future dream.

The future is a little like heaven - everyone wants to go, but not right now. Yet, Danny Cox believes, "Focusing on the future is a guaranteed method of breaking the cycle of stagnation and the habitual ritual of repeating yesterday."

> The trouble with the future is that it usually arrives before we are ready for it.
> —ARNOLD H. GLASOW

The future is your ally. The kind of future we see for tomorrow will shape how we live today. A scary thought struck me recently. What if my future was a repeat of today or, even worse, the past? As important as the past is, I certainly don't want to live there. Dragging around memories of the past, holding on to traditions, or wishing I could relive regrettable moments extinguishes hope for the future. As an unknown author so aptly stated, "The most tiring exercise in the world is carrying yesterday on your back." The past wears us down. You cannot rewrite the past, but the future is yours to be designed.

Here's the key - the future can only provide momentum if you know what you want where you are going. You have to pick a destination. Unless you deliberately point yourself in a specific direction, you'll randomly bump into whatever comes your way.

Several years ago, Northwest Airlines offered some unusual promotional round-trip passagers aboard one of their planes. According to the *Chicago Tribune*, fifty-nine dollars bought a "Mystery Fare" ticket that provided a one-day trip to an unknown American city. Ticket buyers didn't know where their flight would take them until they arrived at the airport the day of the flight. Yet, the airline was flooded with takers. For instance, in Indianapolis fifteen hundred people crowded the airline counter to buy the Mystery Fare tickets that were sold on a first-come, first-served basis.

Not all ticket buyers were thrilled with their mystery destinations. One buyer was hoping for a trip to New Orleans but ended up with a ticket for Minneapolis. He walked through the airport terminal yelling, "I've got one ticket to the Mall of America. I'll trade for anything." Although everyone knew the rules of the game, many built their hopes on glamorous destinations that never materialized.

Mystery Fare tickets is a fun gimmick for a weekend fling, but I wouldn't recommend it as an approach for determining your future destination. Charting a specific course for yourself allows the future to pull you out of the past and into an exciting future of unlimited potential.

Bernard M. Baruch reflected, "I have known personal disappointments and despair. But always the thought of tomorrow has buoyed me up. I have looked to the future all my life. I still do. I believe that with courage and intelligence we can make the future bright with fulfillment." Where do you want to be tomorrow? What do you want to be doing? What are your plans for achieving the important goals in your life? What elements of the past are you holding on to? What are your plans for creating a fulfilling future?

The future is here before you know it. Have you made arrangements to enter it? If not, remember the catchy book title that says, "If you don't know where you're going, you'll probably end up somewhere else."

Enjoy the Journey to Your Purpose

I love the Olympics and must admit I can vegetate several hours in front of the television cheering on our athletes. Every Olympics produces feel good stories and examples of people who overcame incredible odds to perform at the Olympic level.

Speed skater Apolo Anthon Ohno captured the hearts and attention of Olympic enthusiasts with his record setting performance. Before Apolo, there was another great Olympic speed skating story.

When Olympic gold medal speed skater Dan Jansen was nine years old, he was competing at the youth national speed skating championships in Minnesota. His first national title was clearly in sight as he came around a turn and tripped on a rubber hose officials had set up as a lane marker. That single slip cost Jansen the title by one point.

He cried. He cried as his mother removed his skates. He cried during the award ceremonies. He was still crying when he got into the car to return home and continued crying until the family pulled into their driveway six hours later.

Dan's father had remained quiet the entire trip. As they got out of the car, he looked at Dan and said quietly, "You know, Dan, there's more to life than skating around in a circle."

Not bad advice, even for the non-skater. Achieving lofty goals and striving to make our inspiring dreams come true is important. But the real juice, life's defibrillator in the good times and bad, is experienced much less in the result of our efforts than in the process of living itself.

I know we are taught in countless ways to value the completed product, the trophy, the finish line, achieving first place. Just how many of those mountaintop experiences have you had in the last thirty days? Most of us are never going to win a gold medal. Our accomplishments are rarely applauded by huge crowds on a daily basis. Being on the cover of a major magazine is probably beyond our reach.

Measuring life ONLY by our achievements can leave one's heart with an erratic, unfulfilled beat. I know this is blatantly obvious yet subtly mysterious. **How it feels to be alive is the ultimate measuring stick.**

Psychologist William Moulton Marston once wrote in *The Rotarian* that in two years he'd managed to ask approximately 3,000 people. "What do you live for?" About 2,800 of them--more than nine out of ten of them--confessed in various degrees, that they were merely enduring their present lives, hoping for some perfect future not clearly determined and less astutely planned. If you're still waiting for that perfect Utopia life, not enjoying your present life, then you will probably not enjoy life any more if your life were to improve.

This is important! If you think you need a missing piece in order to feel fulfilled, satisfied and capable of living over the edge, you will still feel incomplete, no matter what you acquire or achieve. People who live their lives to the fullest simply get up in the morning and can't wait to start all over again.

"Excuse me," said one bird to another. "You are older, more mature and experienced than I and can no doubt help me. Tell me, where can I find this thing they call the sky? I've been flying around searching for it everywhere."

"The sky?" answered the seasoned bird. "You are flying in it right now."

You are immersed in life. Everything you need is at your disposal and the choices you make today will determine the future you experience. Just like the bird, you are surrounded by the necessary factors for enjoying the process of living.

The irony of this is that people who cherish the "process" of living often experience victories. Dan Jansen for instance. Disappointed at the 1984 Olympics, again in 1988 after learning about the death of his sister who had been fighting leukemia for more than a year, he then struggling with a final turn in 1992 and finished out of the medals in fourth place.

At his fourth Olympic experience in 1996, Dan was expected to win the coveted gold in the 500 meters. He had already been a record-setter in the past and this was his specialty race. Again, tragedy struck. He didn't fall, but in the beginning of the final turn, he lost control of his left skate momentarily, slowing him down just enough to finish in eighth place. It must have been pretty difficult to put his father's advice into perspective. "You know, Dan, there's more to life than skating around in a circle."

One race remained. The 1,000 meter. No matter what, Dan Jansen planned to retire. At the midway point of the race, the clock showed he was skating at a world-record pace, and the crowd sensed the significance and tension in this final race. They cheered and shared the experience with him. When Dan Jansen crossed the finish line, a WR appeared beside his name on the scoreboard—world record. Dan Jansen had finally won that elusive gold medal. His Olympic futility ultimately ended in triumph.

This message is for everyone. It is written as a gentle reminder that quality of life, sensitivity to the splendors of everyday living, and the excitement of feeling fully alive are available to all. You will not be immune from disappointments, periodic failures, or even slipping on the final turn of a successful venture. People special to you will die, your dreams will be thwarted, and your goal may at times appear unattainable.

But, you persevere. Why?

Here's the reality check. Life is not a spectator sport. After you find that one thing that you really want in life, you have to get into the circle and skate. One day, you too will experience the triumph.

CHAPTER 3

LIVE LIFE TODAY

A FTER YOU GET a handle on that "one thing" that you were born to do, your life will begin to make its journey toward that priority. It's important to know where you're going, but it's equally important to live life today.

Actor and film producer Michael Landon said, "Somebody should tell us right at the start of our lives that we are dying. Then we might live life to the limit, every minute of every day. Do it! I say. Whatever you want to do, do it now! There are only so many tomorrows."

THERE ARE ONLY SO MANY TOMORROWS

There is a wonderful scene in the movie *Dead Poet's Society* where Mr. Keating is escorting his group of sophisticated, uptight, adventure-impoverished students to the school's trophy case displays. Photos of earlier graduating classes are prominently displayed.

"Look at these pictures, boys," Keating challenges. "The young men you behold had the same fire in their eyes that you do. They planned to take the world by storm and make something magnificent of their lives. That was years ago.

Now the majority of them are pushing up daisies. How many of them really lived out their dreams? Did they do what they set out to accomplish?" Then, with a dramatic move, Keating leans into his astounded class and passionately whispers, "Carpe diem! Seize the day!"

Contrast that attitude with the one depicted in the classic comedy movie *Groundhog Day* starring Bill Murray. In the movie, Murray repeatedly wakes up at the exact same time on the exact same day. Every day is the same *Groundhog Day* – which he lives over and over again.

That script not only made for good humor, it also depicts the lifestyle of many people. They rise at the same time, eat the same thing for breakfast, head for work at the same time, slide into their comfortable work habits, punch out and head for home. Then, repeat the same thing again tomorrow.

HAPPINESS IS LIVING EVERY MOMENT

Dennis Wholey, author of *Are You Happy*, reported that according to expert opinion, perhaps only 20 percent of Americans are happy. In another national survey, it was estimated that 29 percent of us are happy. That's sad. I'm a pretty happy guy and find it difficult to accept this 'happiness data'.

Regardless of the accuracy of these statistics, there is a pretty good indication that people want more in their lives. There is a hole somewhere waiting to be filled and thereby producing unhappiness. Actually, unhappy people simply have a gap between what they expect and what they are experiencing. That's why happiness has very little to do with what we attain. The more we get, the higher our expectations and the more likely a larger gap will be created.

Former child star Shirley Temple Black told a story about her husband, Charles, and his mother. When Charles was a boy, he asked his mother what the happiest moment of her life was.

"This moment—right now," she responded.

"But what about all the other happy moments in your life?" he asked. "What about when you were married?"

> To experience happiness we must train ourselves to live in this moment, to savor it for what it is, not running ahead in anticipation of some future date nor lagging behind in the paralysis of the past.
>
> —LUCI SWINDOLL

"My happiest moment then was then," she answered. "My happiest moment now is now. You can only really live in the moment you're in. So to me, that's always the happiest moment."

I love Ms. Black's perspective. Whenever you focus on the past, you strip the present of its beauty. And when you get caught up in the future, you rob the present of its potential.

Happiness seems so simple—and yet, so difficult to define. Here's a little help in developing the attitudes that nurture the seeds of happiness.

Accept life's difficulties. I know you know this, but

let me remind you that life will never be void of problems. Pain and difficulty are constantly perched at your back door. They are inevitable experiences of living in an imperfect world. A great starting point to happiness is to accept these unpleasantries as quickly as you do the joys. To be content in the ups and downs of life epitomizes a truly happy person.

Choose happiness now. Waiting for your life to be totally in order before experiencing happiness is an unrealistic dream. "If only" and "Someday I'll" are detours to happiness. They snuff out contentment. The best part of your life is right now, not some day in the past or future. Life may not be as good as you want or as good as you ought to try to make it. But, you really have it pretty good. Learn to be happy with what you have while you pursue all that you want.

Learn to look for the good. Try looking for the positives in your job, relationships, community, church, and family. Guard against focusing on the negatives or things that fall short of your expectations. Identify the little things that bring you a sprinkle of happiness. You'll be pleasantly surprised how developing a mind-set that looks for the good prepares you to deal more positively with the problems you encounter.

Help others experience happiness. Bertrand Russell once said, "If there were in the world today any large number of people who desired their own happiness more than they desired the unhappiness of others, we could have a paradise in a few years." Let go of judging. Accept people where they are. Expect the best from others. Help people believe in themselves. Become an inverse paranoid. You read that right. Inverse paranoids are people who think everyone is out to make them happy. Just imagine everyone you meet wanting to bring happiness to your life. And then try to do the same for them.

Decide what you want in life. In the early 1980s, two Harvard psychologists completed a study of people who called themselves happy. And what did happy people have in common? Money? Success? Power? Health? Love?

None of the above.

Happy people had only two things in common: They knew exactly what they wanted and they felt they were moving toward getting it. Dr. Benjamin Spock concurred. He said, "Happiness is mostly a by-product of doing what makes us feel fulfilled." The ultimate in personal happiness is to be actively involved in something bigger than ourselves that causes us to stretch beyond where we are.

> You are at the top when you have made friends with your past, and you are focused on the present and optimistic about your future.
> —Zig Ziglar

On the flip side, unhappiness can be experienced by not knowing what we want and working like crazy to get it. "Many persons have the wrong idea of what constitutes true happiness," advised Helen Keller. "It is not attained through self-gratification but through fidelity to a worthy purpose."

As Harold Kushner wrote in the best-selling book, *When All You've Ever Wanted Isn't Enough*, "Happiness is a butterfly—the more you chase it, the more it flies away from you and hides. But stop chasing it, put away your net and busy yourself with other, more productive things than the pursuit of happiness and it will sneak up on you from behind and perch on your shoulder."

If you really want to be happy, the only person that can stop you is you. Don't strive to be happy. Be Happy. Wake up each morning. Smile. Look for the good in the day. Choose to act happy.

Remember the infamous words of Erma Bombeck, "Seize the moment. Remember all those women on the Titanic who waved off the dessert cart."

Life isn't intended to be an all-or-nothing fight between winning and losing, misery and bliss, boredom and excitement. Life isn't inherently good or bad. Life is life. Sometimes it's okay, sometimes it's invigorating. Sometimes comfortable. Sometimes unpleasant. Always inviting us to make the most of it.

What a great human being you'll become when you endorse the principle that at the closing of each day you're content with the way you lived it. Seize The Day!

CHAPTER 4

ACQUIRE AN AWESOME ATTITUDE

Have you ever given much thought to the negative people you encounter and the potential impact or influence they have on your life? Let me tell you about one such experience.

"Good morning Ladies and Gentlemen! Welcome aboard United Express Flight 5362 to Chicago. Before we take off, please make sure that your seat backs and tray tables are in their full upright position, and that your seat belts are securely fastened. This is a non-smoking flight and we remind you that smoking in the lavatories and tampering with smoke detectors is prohibited. Buckle up; have a pleasant trip and a nice day."

"They expect me to have a pleasant trip flying in this puddle-jumper?" the passenger next to me blurted.

"This plane is a sorry excuse for a jet," she continued. "I can't believe I paid to ride this thing just to spend a week with my mother-in-law. Oh well, we'll probably never arrive anyway."

Biting my tongue, I smiled and nodded only to acknowledge I had heard her. I waited to suggest to my flying friend that her chances for having a super day were slim to none. Besides that, I sympathized with the mother-in-law having to endure her stay.

She continued entertaining me throughout the flight with everything that was wrong with her life. I just kept smiling and graciously nodding. When the plane landed, I assisted her with the luggage in the overhead compartment and struggled to restrain myself from giving her a bit of advice about life. Instead, I smiled and encouraged her to make it a great day.

I thought to myself walking through the terminal, "Could it be this person was not aware of her negativity? Was she really that fatalistic about her life? Surely she didn't intend to let this flight dictate the quality of her day."

This lady was apparently unaware that she had given control of her day to an airplane she didn't like.

A friend told me about a man who shouted the same three words each day from his street-corner newsstand. "Ain't it awful!" he would say to each passerby while extending a newspaper. People bought a paper because they just had to know what terrible thing had occurred. People are attracted to, love to talk about and dwell on the "awful".

Tragedy and dire predictions always make the front page, but if we become preoccupied with bad news, undesirable circumstances and unfortunate life events, we will succumb to a lifestyle of "awfulizing" – a pervasive pessimism that clouds every situation with gloom.

Charles Swindoll calls this "verbal pollution," passed around by grumblers, complainers, and criticizers. "This poison of pessimism," Swindoll writes, "creates an atmosphere of wholesale negativism where nothing but the bad side of everything is emphasized."

I've been a fan of the Peanuts cartoon for many years. Charles Schulz had the uncanny ability to capture real life messages inside his characters. I recall one strip in which Lucy announces: "Boy, do I feel crabby."

> It's not your position in life – it's the disposition you have which will change your position.
> —Dr. David McKinley

Her loving little brother Linus, always anxious to relieve tension at home, responds, "Maybe I can be of help. Why don't you just take my place here in front of the TV while I go and fix you a nice snack? Sometimes we all need a little pampering to help us feel better." Then Linus brings her a sandwich, a few chocolate chip cookies, and some milk.

"Now is there anything else I can get you?" he asks. "Is there anything I haven't thought of?"

"Yes, there's one thing you haven't thought of," Lucy answers. And then suddenly screams, "I don't want to feel better!"

Lucy never wanted to experience change in her life where bad attitudes were present. It was more "fun" to wallow in her misery.

I've come to the profound, undisputable (in my mind) conclusion; there are a lot of Lucys in this world.

Many people are one positive attitude away from having a great day, pursuing a dream or rebuilding a relationship.

For those people who need a few bullet points or specific strategies, here you go. . .

First, **expect the best**. Seriously, people who expect things to always go bad will not be disappointed. A positive 'expector' adjusts your view on life and allows you the flexibility to enjoy the blessings and deal with challenges. These people are commonly known to be "inverse paranoids". This is someone who believes that the world is conspiring to do him good. How refreshing!

> The optimist pleasantly ponders how high his kite will fly; the pessimist woefully wonders how soon his kite will fall.
> —WILLIAM ARTHUR WARD

Next, **decide to be cheerful**. I tend to respond to the request "How are you?" with "Wonderful" or "Fantastic". Periodically, someone will say, "You can't always be fantastic." True. But I choose to believe I will be any minute.

Cheerfulness, and its negative counterpart, is normally visible on someone's face. When I was in the second grade, I had a fabulous teacher. Mrs. Krull was better to me than I deserved. I think it's because she lived across the alley from my grandparents. She was also a strong disciplinarian. One day during recess, Randy and I were pestering the girls. Mrs. Krull approached us and said, "Boys, when I was a child, I was told that if I made ugly faces, my face would freeze, and I would stay like that."

I was appalled at the potential outcome. However, Randy looked intently for a moment and then said to Mrs. Krull, "Well, teacher, you can't say no one warned you."

Looking downtrodden, depressed, negative, bitter, gloomy, discouraged, apathetic, resentful, and hopeless is pitiful. Smile! Be cheerful! By the time you're 30, you wear the face you deserve.

Be a solution finder. Problem finders are a dime a dozen. Rare are those people who can spot a solution in every problem rather than a problem in every solution. Like the old saying goes, "When you change the way in which you see things, the things you see will change." It's amazing how the slight shift in your perspective on things will alter habitual attitudes.

Talk positive. Listen carefully to your conversations. The words you use, the tone of your voice and your non-verbals not only communicate your attitude to others but further ingrain your personality characteristics. Psychologist Shad Helmstetter advised, "You can't change from a negative mind-set to a positive mind-set without changing from negative talking to positive talking. To do that you must change the input from negative to positive."

Develop a spirit of understanding and acceptance. Look around you. People who display a genuine, caring attitude and love for people normally display an affirmative, upbeat attitude.

John Maxwell tells the story of a mother and her adult daughter shopping one day, trying to make the most of a big sale the weekend before Christmas. As they went from store to store in the mall, the mother complained about everything: the crowds, the poor quality of the merchandise, the prices, and her sore feet. After the mother experienced a particularly difficult interaction with a clerk in one department store, she turned to her daughter and said, "I'm never going back to that store again. Did you see the dirty look she gave me?"

The daughter answered, "She didn't give it to you, Mom. You had it when you went in!"

Ouch! Your attitude toward the people around you will determine the attitude they have toward you which impacts the attitude you have toward life which...you get the message.

Act as if. Act 'as if' you have a great attitude. Act like the kind of day you want to have. Act like the person you want to become. Act like the attitude you want.

One of the most important choices you make today is your attitude. You and you alone are in charge. This is the greatest day of your life. Do something positive with it – acquire an awesome attitude.

CHAPTER 5

NO TOUCH UP NEEDED

I SMILED TO MYSELF as I read the physical description of the newest Barbie being produced. In an attempt to represent all those people with less than fantasy figures, the giant toy maker Mattel introduced a more realistic Barbie. A softer hairstyle, smaller bust line, larger waist and smaller hips were featured on this special edition.

I smiled even more when the *Wall Street Journal* decided to herald Barbie's changes on its front page. Maybe it says something about the fascination we have with glamour, physical perfection, and image. We must, or why would a Barbie sell every two seconds? The average American girl owns eight, and more than 1 billion have been sold since her birth in 1959.

How about a 'real world' application? Instead of comparing ourselves to a perfect specimen, plastic or not, we should view ourselves in terms of our own abilities, special attributes and even our less than perfect characteristics. To admire and fantasize about perfection is an exhausting activity not even capable of producing microscopic change.

A magazine cover featured a picture of Michele Pfeiffer

and the caption read, "What Michele Pfeiffer Needs Is... Absolutely Nothing!" *Oh really?*

It was later discovered that Michele Pfeiffer did need a little help to appear perfect on the magazine's cover. She needed over $1500 worth of touch-up work on that cover photo.

How easy it is to compare ourselves with the media stars, Barbie, or even Mary or Jim down the street who appear to be the perfect specimens of humankind. Consider this thought: each of us was perfectly designed by the Master Creator. And yes, in the eyes of the world, some people are more blessed than others. It's all a matter of perspective.

Self -acceptance makes it possible for you to feel comfortable with the reality that you project on the outside what you feel on the inside. Accepting who you are right now sets the stage for you to upgrade those areas needing a bit of attention. Without acceptance, self-pity and a defeatist attitude will permeate our lives and make personal development virtually impossible.

Denis Waitley says, "It's not what you are that holds you back, it's what you think you're not."

Think about it.

BUILD A BETTER YOU

Do you have a deep down feeling of your value and worth? Do you have an accepting attitude about yourself the way you are? Do you recognize the good and potential within you? Your honest and sincere response to these questions will be an excellent indicator of how your life works out.

The most important opinion you have is the one you believe about you. Ultimately, no one else can determine your self-worth. No one else is accountable for how you feel about you. Therefore, no one's opinion about you is as important as yours.

Dr. Joyce Brothers says, "An individual's self-concept affects every aspect of human behavior: the ability to learn... the capacity to grow and change... the choice of friends, mates and careers. It is no exaggeration to say that a strong positive self-image is the best possible preparation for success in life."

People with a healthy self-concept are able to develop and maintain successful relationships. Their upbeat approach to life also draws uplifting people into their lives.

> I don't think of myself as a poor deprived ghetto girl who made good. I think of myself as somebody who from an early age knew I was responsible for myself, and I had to make good.
> —OPRAH WINFREY

It is impossible to perform consistently in a manner inconsistent with the way you see yourself. Performance is a reflection of internal worth and the true picture you have of yourself. When you are comfortable with yourself, it is natural to feel satisfaction from and enjoy the accomplishments you experience.

What you picture yourself to be, you become. How you

see yourself will determine how you think, feel, act, and react to others. What you display to the world on the outside is a direct reflection of how you feel on the inside. In order to change outward actions, it is necessary to change the inward perception of self. You put a rope around your neck every time you base that perception on anything outside of what you think.

Listen to Norman Vincent Peale's encouragement: "Believe in yourself. Have faith in your abilities! Without a humble but reasonable confidence in your own powers you cannot be successful or happy." Peale is right. Reasonable confidence or competence is a self-fulfilling prophecy we live out, based upon the image we have of ourselves in any given area.

> We cannot love others until we love ourselves. We cannot love ourselves until we truly believe that God loves us.
> —KATHIE LEE GIFFORD

I ran across a poem many years ago that I've carried in my mind and frequently repeat to audiences as well as myself. It goes like this:

God said, "Let's build a better world."
And I said "How?"
The world is such a cold dark place
And so complicated now.
I'm so afraid and helpless,
There's nothing I can do.
But God, in all His wisdom said,
"Just build a better you."

One of the most exciting adventures in your life is to "build a better you." In so doing, your self-confidence will blossom, and you will create more meaning in your life and in the lives of others.

Self-confidence isn't something you can merely talk yourself into. Your worth is firmly in place no matter what you think. Learning to build a stronger self-confidence can be cultivated by tapping into your internal treasure. Consider these building blocks for attaining a healthy level of self-confidence in your life. Check those items where special attention is needed.

- Stop Tearing Yourself Down
- Don't Compare Yourself With Other People
- Make A List Of Your Abilities, Strengths And Talent. Spend 80% Of Your Time Building On These Qualities
- Stop Comparing What You Are To What You Think You Should Be
- Stop Allowing Others To Make You Feel Inferior
- Become An Expert At What You Do
- Initiate A Self-improvement Program
- Set Plans And Goals For The Future Rather Than Worrying About It
- Stop Dwelling On How You Think Others See You
- Help Others Feel Better About Themselves
- Like Yourself

- View Your Mistakes As An Opportunity To Grow And Learn New Ways Of Doing Things
- Don't Let What You Don't Have Prevent You From Using What You Do Have
- Associate With People Who Make You Feel Good About You
- Eliminate Destructive Habits
- Forgive Others And Eliminate Grudges
- Make A Success List Of Your Big And Small Accomplishments
- Find Your Uniqueness And Begin Celebrating It Today
- Don't Settle For A Mediocre You Think about what you can do to build a better you.

LIKE YOURSELF

We normally communicate our level of self-confidence to other people by:

1. The way we look
2. How we act
3. What we say
4. What we do

If you look self-confident and act self-confident, you will gain healthy self-confidence.

Speak clearly. Take pride in how you look, how you

dress, and how you think. Sit straight, walk tall. Walk with confidence. Greet others with a friendly smile and look them directly in the eye. Answer the phone pleasantly.

ASSOCIATE WITH PEOPLE WHO MAKE YOU FEEL GOOD ABOUT YOU

There aren't many things in this world more important than being friends with people who make you feel good about you. Most of us take those relationships for granted and sometimes forget the best way to make friends with people like this is to be that kind of friend to others.

Strive to be someone who lifts others up, encourages them to be their best, and set an example that will inspire others. Be sensitive and responsive to the dreams and ambitions to which others aspire. Show appreciation and celebrate the achievements of others. Be tolerant of weaknesses, listen with understanding, and pick people up when they falter.

It is important to be that type of person to others because we tend to attract that which we are. Secondly, we need to be careful about the type of people with whom we associate.

Stay away from negative people. Steer clear of whiners, complainers, excuse makers, and people who believe it is their responsibility to put you in your place. They don't pay your bills, but they can be costly to your self-confidence.

Adults often talk about peer pressure as it relates to youth. Every parent knows the impact peer pressure has on kids and we frequently preach to our children the importance of choosing good friends. Yet, I fear adults have forgotten that peer pressure does not end after adolescence. Human nature responds to the company it keeps.

Most of us would be wise to take an inventory of our closest friends and acquaintances. Ask yourself, "When I am with this person, do I feel like the most important person in their life?" You'll discover who the people are that you want and should spend time with.

> You'd better learn how to like yourself, because you're going to be spending a lot of time with you.
> —JERRY LEWIS , THE NUTTY PROFESSOR

Accept compliments from other people. Simply respond to compliments with, "Thank you very much." Don't downplay those positive strokes. Only self-confident people can accept compliments with grace. Give yourself a compliment daily, even if no one else does. These are all simple ways of sending a message that you like you.

An action step to building self-confidence is to act as if you have it. Determine now that everything you do in private or public, say to yourself or others, think out loud or think to yourself will reflect an attitude of self-acceptance and self-confidence.

When someone shakes your hand, give them eye contact, a smile and a firm handshake in return. When someone greets you, return the greeting with a positive and firm response. Don't be afraid to admit when you don't know an answer, or have made a mistake, or need additional time to complete a task. Say "I'm sorry" without beating yourself up. Don't let the energy suckers in your life determine your view of you. Instead, inject a healthy dose of confidence into you by 'acting like you like yourself'.

Consider the recommendation of Buck Rogers, "If the package or image you're presenting to the public suggests that you're not sold on yourself, you might consider some redecorating."

CHAPTER 6

CHANGES, CHALLENGES AND CHOICES

L IFE IS FILLED with changes, challenges, demands, pressures, and a host of other unavoidable dilemmas. That's reality! But there are a few character choices that will take you through the toughest of times.

CHOOSE TO RISE ABOVE LIFE'S UNCERTAINTIES

Choosing to rise above the circumstances is powerful and greatly affects the outcome of the day's activities. It's not the events that mold your life, determine your feelings, or guide your actions. Rather, it is the way you decide to interpret and respond.

We must be convinced that we actually have the ability to choose our responses. The value, power, and impact of any life event are determined by your response. Unfortunately, there are many who have conditioned themselves to practice just the opposite.

Be careful not to allow yourself to be victimized by the society in which you live. It's not the culture, the times, the social circumstances. When we blame these elements for our conditions, we return to them for the answers and are continually disappointed. This is the fast track to "victim-itis".

Another roadblock to life by choice is assigning undue control to inherited traits. These people are convinced the quality of their lives have been predetermined through some "gene-o-matic" or DNA mixer. There is no doubt that our social and family conditioning impact each of us, but I would be quick to contend each of us possesses the ability to rise above those influences.

> One's philosophy is not best expressed by words. It is expressed in the choices one makes. In the long run - we shape our lives and we shape ourselves. The process never ends until we die. And the choices we make are our responsibility.
> —ELEANOR ROOSEVELT

I like what Arnold J. Toynbee said, "As human beings, we are endowed with freedom of choice and we cannot shuffle off our responsibility upon the shoulders of God or nature. We must shoulder it ourselves. It is up to us."

CHOOSE TO WALK AWAY FROM ANGER

Anger is a choice! An old adage reminds us that nothing cooks your goose quicker than a boiling temper.

I've been hanging out in a lot of airports recently. Airports have to be one of the angriest places I visit. People are angry because they miss a flight, angry because a flight has been cancelled, angry because they were not chosen to fly standby, angry because they didn't receive the upgrade they requested, or whatever. It's better to abandon a quarrel before it breaks out, even if that quarrel is simply thoughts that are stewing inside of you.

An ancient legend says that Hercules became irritated by a strange-looking animal that blocked his path in a threatening manner. In anger, he struck it with his club. As he went on his way, he encountered the same creature again several times, and in each instance, the beast grew larger and more fearsome than before. At last, a "heavenly messenger" appeared and warned Hercules to stop his furious assaults, saying, "The monster is Strife and you are stirring it up. Just let it alone, and it will shrivel and cease to trouble you."

> The trouble with flying into a rage is that the visibility is poor.
> —ANONYMOUS

Behaviors prompted by anger often create heightened bitterness, strife, and opposition. Both the angered and the aggressor are smitten. Walking away or refusing to dwell on and attack that which angers, provides a logical approach for resolution.

There are also physical reactions to anger. It upsets your normal digestion. It keeps your body from assimilating and eliminating properly because anger causes the blood vessels to constrict. At the same time, it sends a dangerous supercharge of blood to the heart, brain, lungs, and large muscles. It also causes your eyes to dilate.

I can think of very little good that ever comes from anger. It is an incredibly destructive emotion that can be controlled or eliminated if you desire.

Recognize first of all that anger comes from within. It isn't the circumstance, person or words that cause the anger. No one has the power to make you angry. Anger is a choice. Decide to be calm, rational, positive, or allow anger to take its destructive course.

Anger is frequently caused by a disparity of expectations. It is an emotional reaction when things don't work out the way we had planned, when people don't behave the way we expect, or life presents one of its 'surprises'. Fear is also a frequent precipitator of anger.

Change the way you think about life's inevitable ups and downs. Change your attitude about the need for people to meet your expectations. Take control of unbridled emotions and decide how you will respond in any given situation. Melt your defensive tendencies and seek peaceful remedies to interpersonal clashes.

> It's wise to remember that anger is just one letter short of danger.
>
> —SAM EWING

After her daughter got upset with a friend, an Australian mother took the girl aside and offered this life-changing wisdom:

> "Always remember," she said, "anyone who angers you, owns you."

This little girl was Sister Kenny, who later allowed compassion rather than anger help her minister to millions of polio victims through the Sister Kenny Foundation.

CHOOSE TO LAUGH

One of the ways we can "unlearn" angry reactions is to loosen up—laugh a bit more. Many of us have become far too serious. Smiles, chuckles, and belly laughs have been replaced with flat expressions, stomach pains, and ulcers. As Erma Bombeck says, "We sing 'make a joyful noise unto the Lord' while our faces reflect the sadness of one who has just buried a rich aunt who left everything to her pregnant hamster."

Laughter is a cheap medicine. It distracts your attention, changes attitude and outlook of life, causes relaxation and reduction of tension, while increasing the body's natural pain killers.

Dr. Norman Cousins, in his best-selling book, *Anatomy of an Illness As Perceived By the Patient*, takes an interesting look at the use of humor to overcome a painful and debilitating illness. Cousins found that ten minutes of good belly laughter gave him two hours of pain-free sleep. Prior to that, even his heavy medications were unable to relieve the pain enough for him to sleep.

Cousins stumbled upon this phenomenon through happenstance. Doctors applied every medical technology they knew of. No relief. One day he came upon a letter from a consulting doctor who had written Cousins' personal physician. One line in that letter caught his attention. It read, "I'm afraid we're going to lose Norman." Cousins said, "At that point, I began to take more of an interest in the case."

In cooperation with his physician, Cousins began a consistent treatment of Vitamin C along with prescribed humor therapy. He would watch his favorite humorous movies and read funny books. Ten minutes of this unique prescription allowed him two hours of pain-free living. Cousins eventually recovered and in response to his experience, numerous studies have confirmed the value of laughter in healing.

Cousins also commented on another benefit of laughter. "I've never known a person," he said, "who possessed the gift of hearty laughter to be burdened by constipation." Sounds like a beneficial outcome to me.

So how do we improve our LAUGHTER QUOTIENT?

1. BE WILLING TO LAUGH AT YOURSELF.

For you straight-faced, sourpuss, solemn folk, who firmly believe you have nothing to laugh at, read this next sentence carefully. Take off all of your clothes—that's right—strip naked. Now stand in front of a mirror and sing to yourself. If that doesn't draw so much as a chuckle, get out your high school yearbook. Maybe you'll be able to manage a smile or two by reminiscing and seeing how silly you really looked.

How about the short man who quit wearing cowboy

boots? He kidded others that the boots gave him a rash...under his armpits. Some people who are shorter in stature might prefer the term "vertically challenged".

Think of all the failures, stumbling blocks, embarrassing moments, and down-right stupid things you've experienced. Now recall how six months later, you laughed about them (or should have).

Blessed are they who can laugh at themselves. They shall never cease to be entertained.

2. THINK FUNNY.

Even our stressful experiences produce laughter material. It is important to remember that what we think about during those events will determine our reaction.

Take the guy who entered the doctor's examining room and exclaimed, "Sorry I didn't come sooner, Doc, but I got held up in your waiting room."

LIGHTEN UP...THINK FUNNY!

3. LISTEN FOR LIFE'S LAUGHABLE MOMENTS.

Making the most of this free, lawful, healthy gift requires keen listening. Believe me; you must "hear" this conversation in your mind to experience the humor.

You are working in a school cafeteria and today is peanut butter and jelly sandwich day. A third grader picking up his lunch declares, "It is about time we get a home cooked meal."

Listen for the subtle, soft, and simple laughter moments.

4. Renew The Child In You.

Pre-schoolers laugh up to 450 times a day (not always appropriately, I'm sure). Adults laugh an average of 15 times a day. Who do you think is healthier?

A Sunday School teacher was quizzing her class about their Old Testament knowledge.

"What do you think Noah did all that time he was on the ark?" she asked. There was silence. "Do you think he did a lot of fishing?"

"What?" sneered one boy, "With only two worms?"

Children may not find everything funny, but they have the uncanny ability to make anything funny.

As you observe and experience life, ask yourself, "How would a nine-year-old respond?" Even if you don't laugh, the exercise will brighten what you see.

Choose carefully whom you spend your time with because there is a good chance you will take on the qualities, mannerisms, and attitudes of those with whom you associate. Hang out with people who are more like you would like to be. Work at being a builder, not a destroyer, of the human spirit.

Changes, challenges, and choices all have the capacity to impact the quality of our lives. Zig Ziglar was so right. "Keep in mind you're free to choose," he said "but the choices you make today determine what you will be, do and have tomorrow."

CHAPTER 7

NAVIGATING THROUGH
THE HARD TIMES

HARD TIMES COME to us in life. Sometimes we simply fall into a rough patch that really isn't anyone's fault at all. Other times we make mistakes—some that are easily fixed and others that try to grab us by the throat and hang on. Then there's the day-to-day "hard times" of dealing with the stress that comes with giving our best to our family, friendships, and profession. But even in the hard times, it's vital to remember that life is a gift, and we need to play the hand that's dealt to us.

FALLEN ON ROUGH TIMES

On 10:32 Saturday morning, Larry approached our table in Bryant Park in New York City. "I'm sorry to bother you," he apologized. "I've fallen on rough times. Could you spare some money?"

"I'm sorry," I said. "I won't give you money, but I'll buy you some breakfast at the La Bain Quotidien coffee shop. Come with me." (It's just across the street from the park where my wife and I had just purchased our morning goodies to enjoy in the park.)

Larry agreed. As we walked he talked. "I lost my job as a security guard and my wife threw me out," he said. "I'm cold. I'm hungry. I have nowhere to go."

I really didn't care about the accuracy of Larry's story. In fact, I could care less if he was lying through his teeth. I had prayed that morning that God would place someone in our path that day who needed to be loved and that I would respond with unconditional love.

We walked and talked. Larry ordered a large coffee and almond pastry. I paid the bill and we parted our ways with a handshake and a mutual "God Bless You."

Later that morning, we walked deep into Central Park in New York City. You've probably seen the bicycle form of transportation in the city. A strong, but normally, naturally thin, muscular person cycles you in a small carriage fit for two.

We took our first ever eight block ride through Central Park to the "Met" (Metropolitan Museum of Art). Omar was our "driver". He had immigrated to the United States – to survive. He was from Mali.

"If you have no money in Mali," Omar said, "you die! I decided to pursue my happiness in America."

"Are you glad you did? Are you happy?" I asked.

"I'm alive," he responded. Wow! That was powerful!

Upon arrival, I paid the hefty bill he announced, along with an appropriate tip for the short, but uphill trek to the museum.

We shook hands and shared a mutual, "God Bless You!"

In 1993, North Carolina basketball coach, Jim Valvano was awarded the Arthur Ashe Award for Courage. He had recently discovered that he had incurable cancer and had been given six months to live. He ended his acceptance speech with these words:

"I urge all of you to enjoy your life, every precious moment on this earth. Spend each day with some laughter. Don't be afraid to feel....to get your emotions going. Be enthusiastic, because nothing great can be accomplished without enthusiasm. Live your dreams."

Whether you can relate to Larry, Omar or if you are privileged to live a run-of-the-mill normal life, Jim Valvano's advice is all inclusive.

> I like living. I have sometimes been wildly, despairingly, acutely miserable, racked with sorrow, but through it all I still know quite certainly that just to be alive is a grand thing.
> —AGATHA CHRISTIE

It's a great day to be alive! Despite the pain, challenges, disappointments, hurts, mysteries, losses—you get the point—I'm blessed to be alive. Thank you Omar, Larry, Jim Valvano and late Presidential Press Secretary James Brady who said, "You gotta play the hand that's dealt you. There may be pain in that hand, but you play it. And I've played it."

FAILURES AND MISTAKES—YOUR OPPORTUNITY TO GROW

Sometimes I can't help myself—I think about all of the lame brain, stupid, regrettable, asinine mistakes I've made. Good grief, it's frustrating to be 'upper middle age' and still make mistakes normally attributable to youth. I guess I'm a slow learner.

Thankfully, Ralph Waldo Emerson helped me put those blunder filled moments into perspective when he wrote: "Finish every day and be done with it. You have done what you could. Some blunders and absurdities no doubt crept in; forget them as soon as you can. Tomorrow is a new day; begin it well and serenely and with too high a spirit to be cumbered with your old nonsense. This day is all that is good and fair. It is too dear, with its hopes and invitations, to waste a moment on yesterdays."

At the end of the day, let the mistakes go. There is just too much good to be experienced to dwell on your inability to be perfect.

> In order to get where you don't know you can go, you have to make mistakes to find out what you don't know.
> —LES BROWN

View mistakes as a closure on one activity, not the demolition of your reputation. It is something you have done or failed to do, not who you are. Don't make excuses. Learn to forgive yourself. It's virtually impossible to change your shortcomings until you accept yourself despite them. Accept responsibility and move on.

"It's not whether you get knocked down," said Vince Lombardi, "It's whether you get up again." Countless numbers of people consider themselves failures because they performed poorly in school, had unsuccessful relationships, failed to make a team, etc. Failing only means you were not totally prepared to meet the challenge at hand. Keep trying. You are never a failure until you completely give up and fail to get up and go at it again.

FINDING FREEDOM FROM FEAR

Several years ago, a local community college contacted me to do a workshop on supervisory skills. I immediately suggested they had the wrong person. "I'm sorry," I remember saying, "I don't do public speaking. I can't even lead a silent prayer in a phone booth... by myself." The conversation ended and I figured that was the last I would hear from them.

Two weeks later, another call came to my office. "Glenn, we would really like for you to do the program. You work with personnel and we know you could offer a lot of insight." What I realized later is that they had probably called a half dozen other people who turned them down and I was the last one on their list.

"How long does the program have to be?" I asked.

"Two days."

"Two days! I don't know 'two days' worth of information about anything."

To make a long story short, I gave in. The next few

months provided considerable learning about the crippling effects of fear. I had heard all of the clichés about fear like, "We have nothing to fear except fear itself," or "Fear is interest paid on a debt you do not owe." Those were empty thoughts as I wrestled with my decision and attempted to write a workshop that I had agreed to do because I wasn't courageous enough to say 'no.'

It's now thirty plus years later. I've conducted a thousand seminars and keynotes to thousands of people, and learned that facing the fear head on allowed me to gain the confidence to not only speak in front of a group, but attempt other things I thought I couldn't do. In addition, I gained valuable insight into fear's personality.

Fear Reproduces Itself. The more I thought about doing the seminar, the more nervous I became. In fact, those feelings carried over into other facets of my life that were normally in my comfort zone.

Fear Breeds Inaction. I had a substantial amount of material to write and organize to insure the workshop's success. Yet, I found myself daydreaming and worrying about the outcome of the program rather than digging in and getting the work done.

Unchallenged fear paralyzes. John F. Kennedy suggested, "There are risks and costs to a program of action, but they are far less than the long-range risks and costs of comfortable inaction."

Fear Snuffs Out Confidence. Amen! I started out with minimal confidence that I could pull off this public speaking commitment. The self-doubt compounded and filtered into more areas of my life.

You can have all the talent in the world, but allowing fear to be in control will squelch your belief in what you can do. If you don't believe you can do something, you will inevitably sabotage your own efforts. It's at this point fear becomes more powerful than our dreams.

Fear Keeps Us From Realizing Our Potential. The only "potential" on my mind for several weeks was the potential public disaster and humiliation I was going to face. Thinking about "being my best" took a back seat to thinking about "surviving".

Fear-strapped people struggle to try new things, dream, excel, and produce beyond their current level of functioning. They live in a relatively small box nailed together by insecurities and covered with the lid of fear.

Eleanor Roosevelt endorsed a novel and effective way of handling the fear of trying something new. She suggested, "Anyone can conquer fear by first doing three things: do it once to prove to yourself that you can do it. Do it a second time to see whether or not you like it. And then do it again to see whether or not you want to keep on doing it." Ms. Roosevelt believed that by the time you've moved through the third step, fear is extinguished. What has changed? Simply, you have handled the fear.

You probably noticed a common theme in this approach -- taking action. There is no victory over fear by sitting in your favorite easy chair and attempting to wish it away. In fact Dale Carnegie believed, "We generate fears while we sit; we overcome them by action. Fear is nature's warning signal to get busy."

Notice that no one suggests you pretend fear doesn't exist. Just the opposite. The first step in overcoming fear's restrictive power is to acknowledge it. Then, Fred Pryor suggests, "One of the best ways to conquer fear is to move toward it." When you find yourself submitting to fear's temptations, remember that we tend to give our fears more power than they deserve. By failing to confront them, we permit them to dominate our lives. The answer? Fears diminish and lose their control and power over you as you confront them.

Take your greatest fear and turn it into a motivator. "The hero and the coward," said boxing manager Cus D'Amato, "both feel exactly the same fear, only the hero confronts the fear and converts it into fire."

You are stronger than your fears or you wouldn't have made it this far.

Hang On To What's Working, Let Go of What Isn't

Thornton Wilder's *Our Town* has a graveyard scene where those who have died are looking back at their lost opportunities. Emily, a young mother who has just died in childbirth, gets a chance to go back in time as an observer at her twelfth birthday. She is astounded by how fast everything is going and how little time there is to enjoy relationships and the little things that mean so much. As she comes back to her grave she says, "I can't go on. It goes so fast. We don't have time to look at one another.... Do any human beings ever realize life while they live it? -- every, every minute?"

That is a provocative question. "Do human beings ever realize life while they live it?" Life is moving at a break-neck speed. If only we could see ahead before we get there to know how life is going to work out. Would it change the way we live now?

What are you doing in your life right now that works? What doesn't work? Are you doing enough of the things that work to move you closer to where you want to be tomorrow? Are you moving forward, standing still, or just spinning in a circle?

It takes a lot of effort not to become a victim of you. Take full responsibility for your life. Make choices that move you closer to where you want to be. Quit doing those things that don't work. Refrain from sitting around with your fingers crossed hoping things will get better. They won't. Not that way. Take full responsibility even for your moments of irresponsibility.

People stuck on bemoaning their lives make a big mistake. They often think people who are really living have a lot more excitement to inspire them. Wrong! They are indulged in mundane activities, have to pay for their groceries, and work to meet the mortgage. In fact, their toilets get clogged and their roofs leak. Their children are not angels and bugs splatter against their windshield. They get holes in the bottom of their shoe soles and cavities in their teeth.

So what's the difference? They keep doing more of what causes them to live above the ordinary.

So, is your life working? If so, keep doing what works and find more ways to do it. If not, accept conditions as they exist or accept responsibility for doing something about it.

Your future need not be a repeat of your past. If your life has been filled with scarcity, competition, or disappointment, there's no reason to convince yourself that your future can't be different.

Past relationships been a bit shaky? Then invest in present relationships the positive qualities and expectations you want future relationships to possess.

Your career has been a drag? What are you investing in it and mentally expecting from it? Step outside of your present position and see what it could become and determine what additional value you can offer.

> You are always only one choice away from changing your life.
> —MARCY BLOCHOWIAK

What are you doing to take charge of your life? Who else is better qualified? You are the lead actor. Are you living by the values you profess? Are your personal priorities given the attention they deserve? If so, you are tapping into an inexhaustible energy source that will help you sustain an energetic, vital and significant life.

Hang on to what works and let go of what isn't working. It's your choice.

MASTERING STRESS

Sometimes it's not the hard times we fall into, but striving to meet the day-to-day challenges that come with giving our best to our family, friendships, and profession. Having said that, "stress" is a used, misused, abused, and overused word in our daily conversations. What really is stress?

Dr. Hans Seyle, the father of stress management research says, "Stress is the wear and tear on your body caused by life's events." It is the body's physical, mental and chemical reactions to circumstances that frighten, excite, confuse, endanger, and irritate.

Hundreds of experiences in life cause stress. These stressors create eustress (good stress) or distress (negative stress). Our bodies are designed to meet these stressors. However, each person must determine what is the right amount of stress for them to function at their optimum level.

> Reality is the leading cause of stress for those in touch with it.
> —JANE WAGNER

Experiencing too little stress causes irritability, boredom, dullness, and apathy. Too much stress can produce comparable results, along with feelings of being overwhelmed.

Dr. Seyle believed the most frequent causes of stress are

an inability to adapt and not having an established code of behavior to guide our actions.

Adapt? In a laboratory experiment, frogs were placed in a shallow pan of room temperature water. They were free to jump out of the pan at will. Under each pan was a Bunsen burner, which heated the water very gradually. As the temperature rose, the frogs adapted. Unfortunately, regardless of how hot the water became, the frogs never became uncomfortable enough to jump out of the pan.

So what happened? The frogs died because they did not have a code of behavior that told them to jump.

Likewise, we need to learn when enough is enough. Adapting is fine, but not without a code of behavior that warns us when it is time to jump. That same code is a warning signal that lets us know it is time to take action to deal with the stressors that now threaten our healthy existence.

> Stress is when you wake up screaming and you realize you haven't fallen asleep yet.
> —ANONYMOUS

Dr. Paul Rosch at the American Institute of Stress says, "The answer to stress management is to realize that stress is an unavoidable consequence of life." Stress is a given in life but the impact on us is determined by how we respond to the experiences that cause stress.

Dealing with stress is an inside job. Adapt to it, learn from it, and enjoy the positive results it can produce, but beware of getting burned by it.

FRESH PAGE!

No matter what your past has been, or what mistakes were made, you have a spotless future. Henry Ward Beecher said, "Every man should be born again on the first day of January. Start with a fresh page. Take up one hole more in the buckle if necessary, or let down one, according to the circumstances; but on the first of January let every man gird himself once more, with his face to the front, and take no interest in the things that were and are past."

The past isn't your present and the present doesn't determine the future. The future is a blank canvas waiting to be fashioned, designed and constructed one piece at a time. The only way to create an original future is to leave the past behind.

The successes, challenges, joys, disappointments, failures and awards of the past are history. Learn from them. Leave them there. Look to the future. This is the time to create your future – you're going to live the rest of your life there.

Don't be like the guy who walked by a little shop with a sign reading "Fortune Teller". Discouraged, disappointed with his past and curious about his life,

> Though no one can go back and make a brand new start, anyone can start from now and make a brand new ending.
> —CARL BARD

he decided to consult with the mystic and ask for a glimpse into his future.

The fortune teller looked into her crystal ball and slowly raised her eyes to meet with her client's.

"What did you see?" he asked.

"You'll be poor, unhappy and miserable until you're fifty."

"Then what?" asked the man with desperation in his voice.

"By that time," the fortune teller said, "you'll get used to it."

The future isn't something to 'get used to'. Determine today that your spotless future will be filled with aspirations, adventures, action, and anticipatory energy. Don't allow the past or the present to sideline your future potential. Let the wisdom of Spanish essayist, novelist, poet, playwright and philosopher (multi-tasker) Miguel de Unamuno rattle your thinking a bit. He asserted, "We should try to be the parents of our future rather than the offspring of our past." Powerful!

It is time! Your best days are still ahead. Create a fresh page. Today.

CHAPTER 8

CELEBRATE! DO THE VICTORY DANCE!

I N THE LATE 1970s, biophysicist Harold J. Morowitz of Yale University reached some astounding conclusions about what it would cost to make a human body. Considering all the proteins, enzymes, RNA, DNA, amino acids, and other complex biochemicals that comprise the human life, Dr. Morowitz concluded, "Fashioning the chemical shopping list into human cells might cost six quadrillion dollars. Assembling the resulting heap of cells into tissue, the tissue into organs, and the organs into a warm body might drain all the treasuries of the world, with no guarantee of success."

No doubt about it; you are a valuable and unique human being. There never has been nor will there ever be anyone like you. Each day we live and breathe on planet earth is one more day to celebrate!

CELEBRATE YOUR UNIQUENESS

I've been going bald or being bald for the greater part of my life. I had friends who were losing their hair in college (like me) and their self-image was devastated by being follicle challenged. I also had a friend who couldn't grow a mustache. Maybe 3 or 4 hairs. He was so bummed he used mascara to fill in his upper lip. Gross. I hated it when he started sweating and his mustache began 'running'. Ugly.

Have you ever wondered why it is so difficult to accept our uniqueness and move on? I even suggest we celebrate the things that make us unique.

My daughter spells her name Katy. In elementary school, a teacher commented how unusual she thought that was. "Most girls I know with your name spell it Katie," she told my daughter. "Yours is different. Why is that?"

"I don't know," Katy responded, "I guess I'm just special." And she is.

> The universe is not going to see someone like you again in the entire history of creation.
> —VARTAN GREGORIAN

Thousands of years ago, a slave named Aesop wrote some simple fables that illustrated certain principles of thought and behavior. They continue to affect people's lives because the applications remain relevant. One such fable is that of the deer and the hunter. The deer was admiring his reflection in the pool.

"Ah", said he, "where can you see such noble horns as these, with such antlers? I wish I had legs worthy to bear such a glorious crown. It is a pity they are so slim and unsightly." At that moment, a hunter appeared and sent an arrow flying toward the deer. The deer bounded off and by means of his nimble legs that he was just complaining about was quickly out of range of the hunter.

Sometimes it's the very quality we don't admire much in ourselves that proves to be the most valuable one we possess. We all have our own uniqueness and they make us special. Like Walt Disney said, "The more you are like yourself, the less you are like anyone else. This is what makes you unique." Don't try covering up your uniqueness, hiding it in a closet or denying it exists. Follow Katy's response each time you are reminded of your uniqueness. "I guess I'm special!"

CELEBRATE SUCCESS

When I say, "Celebrate success," I'm certainly not promoting a lifestyle of arrogance or pride. "When a man is wrapped up in himself," said John Ruskin, "he makes a pretty small package." People who dwell on how good they are and hold their achievements out for the world to pat them on the back are boring, indirectly demeaning (we could never match their achievement) and actually often times insecure (although it may not seem like it).

However, there is room and reason for personal celebration.

My motivation for this suggestion is simple. Sometimes you just need a reminder of the good things you've done, the projects you've completed, the people you've touched, and the goals you've attained. Any achievement, no matter how big or seemingly insignificant, is important to list.

63

Keep your list handy and add to it every time you feel good about an achievement.

Along with being amazed at the successes you've had, you create a foundation for building future successes. By recognizing what you are capable of achieving, you set the wheels in motion to experience future achievement.

> Success can make you go one of two ways. It can make you a prima donna, or it can smooth the edges, take away the insecurities, let the nice things come out.
>
> —BARBARA WALTERS

Don't take any accomplishment lightly. Determine the ability, action and perseverance needed to attain each goal. Briefly pat yourself on the back and set out on your next venture to try new things, take on additional responsibility, and gain valuable experience.

To create your own success inventory, begin by answering these questions:

1. What do I feel good about in my life right now?

2. What have I done in the past six months (personally or professionally) that I'm proud of?

3. What have I done for somebody else in the past month that made me feel good?

4. What do other people tell me makes me unique or special?

Go ahead, put your list together and use it as a private source of inspiration. By creating a list of your positive experiences and successes, the stage is set, your confidence increased, and momentum generated to uncover potential opportunities.

CELEBRATE LIFE

I fear the list of precious, promising, positive, pertinent overlooked good things in my life would be embarrassing. I would have to begin with a renewed thankfulness for the breath of life.

After being diagnosed with terminal cancer, 47-year-old Randy Pausch returned to Carnegie Mellon University, where he taught computer science, to deliver a final lecture to colleagues. The professor hoped 150 people might show up. Instead, the 400-seat lecture auditorium was filled.

Randy Pausch's "last lecture" was delivered in September 2007. The lecture began with him standing before a screen beaming down chilling CT images of tumors in his liver, under the title, **The Elephant in the Room**. He then stunned the audience with this announcement, "I have about six months to live. I'm in really good shape, probably better shape than most of you." He then dropped to the floor to do push-ups.

> The more you praise and celebrate your life, the more there is in life to celebrate.
> —OPRAH WINFREY

Randy opened his heart to the audience in a humorous, insightful, and emotion packed farewell that was more focused on living than on his imminent death. He told his colleagues and students, "I'm dying and I'm having fun, and I'm going to keep having fun every day I have left."

Within weeks, his videotaped lecture was seen by millions on the Internet and later became the material for a bestselling book. Randy Pausch was a dying man who taught those who listened how to live. He died on July 25, 2008 but his legacy, wisdom, wonderful outlook on life and passion remain a living inspiration to us all.

Isn't it amazing how those facing death have an unusually clear perspective on what is truly important in life?

What about us?

What's going right in your life today? What are you thankful for? What are you celebrating? What have you done to make this day the best one you've had in a long time? What relationships are blessing your life? Do you enjoy your work? Your coworkers (have you told them?)

> It ain't no sin to be glad you're alive.
> —BRUCE SPRINGSTEIN

You might have to look around – search a bit to find all of your blessings. I'm convinced there will be some you've overlooked since we have countless things in our lives to be thankful for.

Several years ago actor Bill Murray starred in a movie called Ground Hog Day. In this comedy he had to keep re-living a particular day all over again until things came out right.

I've never been given the chance to relive a day in my

life. If I had to do a day over again, I'm certain I wouldn't take for granted everything I had the day before – or least I think I have enough common sense not to mess it up two days in a row – or maybe not.

Here's an exercise for you. For the next three days keep a written list of everything you have the freedom to enjoy, every potential blessing in the day, every accomplishment, and every relationship that is enriching your life. That intense three day focus might just jumpstart a renewed appreciation for your life.

Jump up! Do the victory dance! There will never be anyone else like you. There will never be another day like today.

Celebrate It!

If you're a fan of this book, please tell others...

- Write about *Celebrate* on your blog. Post excerpts to your social media sites such as: Facebook, Twitter, Pinterest, Instagram, etc.
- Suggest *Celebrate* to friends
- When you're in a bookstore, ask them if they carry the book. The book is available through all major distributors, so any bookstore that does not have it in stock can easily order it.
- Write a positive review on www.amazon.com.
- Purchase additional copies to give away as gifts

You can order additional copies of the book from your local bookstore or from my website by going to www.enthusedaboutlife.com. Special bulk quantity discounts are available.

Check out my other books to help maximize your effectiveness and impact at home, at work in the relationships that matter most...

Tinker

Discover the secrets for achieving excellence in our fast-paced, ever changing, chaotic world.

Playbook

Achieve higher professional results with insights provided in these pages.

To order these books, go to my website: www.enthusedaboutlife.com

ADDITIONAL RESOURCES...

My first three book series can give you 12 simple secrets to a variety of life's goals. To find out more, and order copies, go to www.enthused about life.com

The Speaker's Sourcebook II duo will help you gain confidence in front of a crowd. To find out more, visit www.enthusedaboutlife.com.

Love Is A Verb is about those simple, yet often forgotten, accumulations of little actions that contribute to building our relationships into what we want them to become. To find out more, visit www.enthusedaboutlife.com or www.simpletruths.com.